Loves Embrace

Loves Embrace

Poems of Prayer Hope and Peace
From
Melvinia "Cissy" Patterson Wilson

iUniverse, Inc.

New York Lincoln Shanghai

Loves Embrace

iUniverse books may be ordered through booksellers or by contacting:

iUniverse
2021 Pine Lake Road, Suite 100
Lincoln, NE 68512
www.iuniverse.com
1-800-Authors (1-800-288-4677)

Because of the dynamic nature of the Internet, any Web addresses or links contained in this book may have changed since publication and may no longer be valid.

ISBN: 978-0-595-44655-1 (pbk)
ISBN: 978-0-595-88979-2 (ebk)

Printed in the United States of America

Melvinia "Cissy" Patterson Wilson
Starlight Consulting
Richmond, Virginia, USA

References to the Holy Scriptures—Bibles texts are from King James Version (KJV), the New Revised Standard Version (NRSV) the New International Version (NIV) and the New World Translation of the Holy Scriptures (NWT) are made after each poem and prayer. Some poems from the book, Love's Embrace: Poems of Love and Inspiration are referenced in this book. Illustrations are from the Microsoft Word software copyrighted 2003, and from the Printmaster Silver 12 software copyrighted 2002.

Contents

Proclamation

The poetry in this book was written before I decided to include some of the inspired writings of Jesus, the Christ, the disciples and saints from the Holy Scriptures. It is not my intention to change anything that has been written in the Holy Scriptures. In each statement and in each paragraph of the Holy Scriptures that is referenced, "The Word, The Sword of the Spirit" is under God's Assurance.

I proclaim words from the passage where Jesus was tempted by the devil, "IT IS WRITTEN" three times, KJV (Matthew 4: 1-10, p. 1200). Nothing is to be added, taken away or changed, according to (Jesus) His word, for, "man shall not live by bread alone, but by every word that proceedeth out of the mouth of God." KJV (Matthew 4: 4, p. 1200).

I am,

MELVINIA "CISSY" PATTERSON WILSON

**Whenever you see a rainbow, you will know
that the storm is over, and that the dawn is God's promise of a new day.
Peace be unto you.**

THE LOVE LETTERS

Loves Embrace

"In the beginning God created the heavens and the earth."

—NWT
Genesis 1: 1 p. 7

"Honor your father and your mother, as the Lord your God has commanded you, so that you may live long and that it may go well with you in the land the Lord your God is giving you."

—KJV
Deuteronomy 5: 16 p. 283

"Hear O Israel: The Lord our God, the Lord is one. Love the Lord your God with all your heart and with all your soul and with all your strength. These commandments that I give you today are to be upon your hearts. Impress them on your children. Talk about them when you sit at home and when you walk along the road, when you lie down and when you get up. Tie them as symbols on your hands and bind them on your foreheads. Write them on the doorframes of your houses and on your gates."

—NIV
Deuteronomy 6: 4-9, p. 284

LETTER OF INTRODUCTION AND INVITATION

The contents of this book contain approximately fifty writings, which express themes of love, faith, hope and spiritual understanding. Some are metaphors, expressions of love and light. Some are similes that make you smile as well as spark an internal glow. The prayers and poems are accompanied by the biblical writings of the Divine, written by the prophets of the Old and New Testaments. Some are personal prayers and visions of what God has for me as well as for each of us. There is so much He has already given us. We simply have to recognize each glorious gift as we travel through life and in relationship.

I did not begin to truly know myself and to accept myself as I am, until these special words, these holy words, began to flow from the Almighty into my heart, then from my heart onto paper. I began to experience the joy of Jesus, the Christ in my soul, an inexpressible exuberance and a sense of spiritual freedom I had never known before. And now that I have discovered that I could express this freedom and truly feel happiness by writing about this gift, I can, finally, with courage, express the opposing end of this continuum of sadness and serenity, and recognize that they are one in the same. We must surrender to our pain and sadness in order to experience the joy of Jesus Christ, for He is Lord of all.

This book, <u>Loves Embrace: Poems of Prayer, Hope and Peace</u>, carries a somewhat different meaning from my first book, <u>Love's Embrace: Poems of Love and Inspiration</u>. On my spiritual journey, I have come to know seven loves. Each was one step closer to the Almighty. Throughout my journey in the wilderness of tears and tremendous pain, I have come to know that there is this parallel experience of infinite joy and peace in a time and space that I have not been able to find words to express. Once I experienced the vision of hope for my life, (for I know, by faith that He is going to show you the vision for your own life if you seek Him) and that I was going to make it out of the wilderness. I found that there is truly divine purpose operating at all times in our lives as one comes to know God. Hopefully, this book will assist you along that spiritual path.

I feel that the love we have for each other is an expression of spiritual consciousness. Love, and our ways of expressing love are indicators of how far we are along the path to higher consciousness and spiritual understanding. Regardless of any religious affiliation or spiritual circumstance, I believe we are truly blessed when we love and are loved. This is a spiritual truth of the entire universe. We are love, and we reflect love in every way through our relationships. We mirror love through our gifts of love songs, our paintings of beautiful art, our writings of love and spiritual poetry, even through our freshly baked honey breads and warm smiles. These are all acts of creation, all acts of love, and with these acts of love, there is God. You have no need, as you are acting as a gift of His Divine Presence to others.

"Take the helmet of salvation, and the Sword of the Spirit, which is the Word of God", NRSV (Ephesians 6:17, p. 1070) is the means by which the child of God discerns.

Do not allow anyone to persuade you to feel that man's opinion is necessary for you to make the right judgments, as it is the work of God. "But the Anointing which ye have received of Him abideth in you, and ye need not that any man teach you: but as the same Anointing teacheth you of all things, and is Truth, and is no lie, and even as It [He] hath taught you, ye shall abide in Him", KJV (1 John 2:27, p. 1536).

I invite you to read these writings of hope and salvation, for they are not mine. They belong to the Lord, Jesus Christ and you, who read them, hopefully will experience feelings of blessedness from the time expended. These are messages from God, I believe, given to me to give to you. I hope you will begin to feel the flow of a loving energy (unconditional) that permeates from me to you.

Always in all ways, I know that you are smiling, sisters and brothers throughout God's infinite universe, I love you.

Peace to all.

I am

Melvinia "Cissy" Patterson Wilson

PREFACE

Giving honor to the Almighty Supreme Spirit, Jesus Christ, I am very grateful to be on the earth to learn the great lessons of life, love and light. My feelings of longing began over twenty years ago. It still continues to this day. Through longing I have become closer to God's love, and in knowing that love, that kind of love He has for me and for all of us, I am free. He sets us free, free from the physical plane of falsities, delusions and half-truths. I can close my eyes and see Him coming, riding upon a thunderous cloud, shining as the brightest, most glorious of stars, and as I reach to that bright beautiful star, I recognize my true essence, that is all love.

Loves Embrace: Poems of Prayer, Hope and Peace, is a book about loves, the metaphors for expressions of life and great sacred love from all of God's children, nature and the universe. For God is the true source of love that we are all a part, and He gave his only begotten Son, Jesus to the world to save our souls from condemnation (NIV John the Divine, 3:16, p. 1650).

I hope that you will begin to know this love of Jesus, the Christ, when you begin to question your true purpose here. For I believe your true purpose is usually a great gift that God has already bestowed upon you, and that, He wants you to share that amazing gift with the world. Your gift to the world is usually not studied or attained by earthly means, for it is already inside you when you came here to the Earth. It is a gift that you must discover on your journey of love within, a talent that is only unique to you. So, please begin to read your Bible.

Try to understand its messages with your heart and mind. Have faith that you will receive guidance from the heavenly angels. This could be someone you will meet or that you have already met or has always been there for you.

Trust God and He will show you the way, the truth and the light that you will be reborn into a new level of spiritual consciousness. You will grow to know his tremendous love for you.

I believe that God has given me a gift to share with you. I call it a gift because it is of great value to me, so easy to complete because of its great value to me. Please accept this gift as I have, with grace, thanksgiving and blessing to the world, for we can only attain what we truly value in life, and, love is the key to life's attainment. Be blessed.

WITH SPECIAL ACKNOWLEDGEMENTS TO MY FAMILY

I thank you for your love and for giving me life. May God Bless you all.

ACKNOWLEDGEMENTS

Giving honor to the Almighty Supreme Spirit, Jesus Christ, I am very thankful to be here on the earth today and to learn from the Messiah's lessons of life, love, light and salvation. I express my deepest love and appreciation for all the patience and love that my husband has given me as my lover and partner for twenty years. To my beautiful daughters, who have given me many spiritual gifts as a mother along the way, I thank you. To my son, who was with us for a few precious moments, I thank you. To my mother and father, my sister and brother, with love and kindness, I thank you. In memory of my grandfathers and grandmothers, God Bless you all. To the newest members of our family, my granddaughters, I love you so very much. You are truly the gifts of joy, laughter, innocence and tremendous spiritual renewing of my heart and soul. I know that God has truly loved and forgiven me.

With special acknowledgement to my protectors and advisors who have given me inspiration to write and perform like no other, I love you, my angels. I also would like to express praise and thankfulness to the spiritual guidance of the Lord Jesus Christ. I thank the saints who have protected me and for all of their loving kindness and encouragement and inspiration assisting me in the writing of this book. I am so grateful. Thank you, my enemies, for you have given me the great gift of tremendous strength.

May God continuously send blessings to those who have richly blessed my life and taught me the true spiritual path. I am deeply grateful for your gifts of time.

As I continue to learn and grow in love and light, I will always remember, with each caress of the winds, there is a renewing of the mind, body and spirit as all loves embrace.

THE HOLY
SCRIPTURES AND
POETRY

Loves Embrace

"In the last days, the mountain of the Lord's temple will be established as chief among the mountains; it will be raised above the hills, and all the nations will stream to it. Many peoples will come and say, "Come let us go up the mountain of the Lord, to the house of the God of Jacob. He will teach us his ways, so that we may walk in his paths." The law will go out from Zion, the word of the Lord from Jerusalem. He will judge between the nations and will settle disputes for many peoples. They will beat their swords into plowshares and their spears into pruning hooks. Nation will not take up sword against nation, nor will they train for war anymore. Come O house of Jacob; let us walk in the light of the Lord.

—*NIV*
Isaiah 2: 2-4 p. 476,
and (similar writings) Micah 4: 1-3, p. 647

Love's Embrace

Love is always in the air
Waiting with baited breath,
To grasp your warmest embrace
To feel your calmest caress.

Love is always in the air
Dancing among the galaxies,
Hoping to see your smiling eyes
Searching for celestine ecstasy.

Love is always in the air
Resting upon the cumulus nebula
Waiting for the sweet lips of thunder
To kiss an ear's heart that's hungered.

Love is always in the air
Singing with the blue birds of happiness,
With songs resounding as, "Easter, Easter"
"Tweet, Tweet", Tweet, and the "Cheerful, Cheerful" Giver.

The Holy Scriptures: It is Written

If I speak with the tongues of men and of angels, but have not love, I am become sounding brass, or a clanging cymbal. And if I have [the gift of] prophecy, and know all mysteries and all knowledge; and if I have all faith, so as to remove mountains, but have not love, I am nothing.

And if I bestow all my goods to feed [the poor], and if I give my body to be burned, but have not love, it profiteth me nothing. Love suffereth long, [and] is kind; love envieth not; love vaunteth not itself, is not puffed up, Love never faileth: but whether [there be] prophecies, they shall be done away; whether [there be] tongues, they shall cease; whether [there be] knowledge, it shall vanish away.

—KJV
1 Corinthians 13:1-8, p. 1444

Let love be genuine, hate what is evil, hold fast to what is good; love one another with mutual affection; outdo one another in showing honor; do not lag in zeal, be ardent in spirit, serve the Lord. Rejoice in hope, be patient in suffering, persevere in prayer. Contribute to the needs of the saints, extend hospitality to strangers.

—NRSV
Romans 12:9-13, p. 1764

Seven Steps to Heaven

From faith, there are seven steps,
And the last of these is love.
These are the Christian virtues
That every Christian should have.
Let us climb this stairway together:

The first step is faith
The second step is virtue
The third step is knowledge
The fourth step is self-control
The fifth step is patience
The sixth step is godliness
The seventh step is kindness
And there awaits love.

Guide us Dear Lord, Jesus
As we move along the path,
Experiencing the joys and pains of life
Returning to You, The Cornerstone,
The Almighty, Chosen One.
One step at a time
Never looking back,
But always moving forward
To that special place called
HEAVEN.

The Holy Scriptures: It is Written

Thou wilt show me the path of life: In thy presence is fullness of joy; In thy right hand there are pleasures for evermore.

—*KJV*
Psalm 16:11, p. 741

Then one of the seven angels who had the seven bowls full of the seven plagues came and said to me, "Come, I will show you the bride, the wife of the Lamb." And in the spirit he carried me away to a great, high mountain and showed me the holy city Jerusalem coming down out of heaven from God. It has the glory of God and radiance like a very rare jewel, like jasper, clear as crystal.

—*NIV*
Revelation 21: 9-11, p. 193

The Lord is king; let the peoples tremble! He sits upon the cherubim; let the earth quake!

—*NIV*
Psalm 99: 1, p. 936

Prayer for Love

We ask you, God of Love,
To open our hearts
To give unto us understanding
That the longing we often feel
Is only an experience to guide us
Along our path to You,
The Almighty, Jehovah, God.

Help us to surrender our souls
Completely to you, Dear Lord,
And experience the joy
Of each communication of spirit
As we become one with You, Beloved
In prayer and supplication
In the solice and silence of the garden.

And that all who will raise their heads
With each gaze toward the Heavens,
Will see the glorious light of Holiness
And whisper the peace of your presence
Calming the storms of life
With your everlasting love and assurance
That life is truly worth living
One day at a time with you, Sweet Jesus.
Amen.

The Holy Scriptures: It is Written

The LORD said to him, "I have heard your prayer and your supplication, which you have made before me; I have consecrated this house which you have built by putting My name there forever, and My eyes and My heart will always be there.

—NIV
1 Kings 9:3, p. 538

Beloved, let us love one another, because love is from God; everyone who loves is born of God and knows God. Whoever does not love does not know God, for God is love. God's love was revealed among us in this way: God sent his only begotten Son into the world so that we might live through Him.

—NIV
1 John 4:7-9, p. 1538

For so the Lord has commanded us, saying "I have set you to be a light for the Gentiles, so that you may bring salvation to the ends of the earth"

—NIV
Acts 13:47, p. 1716

Prayer for Healing, Love and Forgiveness

We ask you, Lord, Great Healer
To forgive us for our transgressions
And to open our heart of hearts
To forgive ourselves and others
So we can heal all and be healed.

We ask You, Wonderful Counselor
To love us and protect us
From those strongholds that are
So difficult to overcome,
So that we can become strong
And acknowledge such strength
That is your gift to us.

We ask you, Almighty, Jesus Christ
To have us embrace each essence of love
That finds its way to us
So that we all can experience
That the joys and pains of life
Exist not one without the other.
Amen.

The Holy Scriptures: It is Written

"And when He had entered Capernaum, a centurion came to Him, entreating Him, ^{and} saying, "Lord, my servant is lying paralyzed at home, suffering great pain." And He said to him, "I will come and heal him." But the centurion answered and said, "Lord, I am not worthy for You to come under my roof, but just say the word, and my servant will be healed. "For I, too, am a man under authority, with soldiers under me; and I say to this one, 'Go!' and he goes, and to another, 'Come!' and he comes, and to my slave, 'Do this!' and he does it." Now when Jesus heard this, He marveled, and said to those who were following, "Truly I say to you, I have not found such great faith with anyone in Israel. "And I say to you, that many shall come from east and west, and recline at the table with Abraham, and Isaac, and Jacob, in the kingdom of heaven; but the sons of the kingdom shall be cast out into the outer darkness; in that place there shall be weeping and gnashing of teeth." And Jesus said to the centurion, "Go your way; let it be done to you as you have believed." And the servant was healed that very hour."

—*NIV*
Matthew 8:5-13, p. 1506

Every Prayer

Every prayer to God is answered
Don't be discouraged or disillusioned
About what is or could have been
For faith is the key to our movement,

Along our path to the Supreme Being
Our hopes and fears to question
It is the only way to learn
That the answer is in the asking,

So don't forget to look to the past
From where you have started
To see how far you've come
To know that God is eminent,

In His Blessed Assurance
That we are not alone
In this vast universe
Pray to Him and see
The miracles of His presence.

The Holy Scriptures: It is Written

"Finally, my brethren, be strong in the LORD, and in the power of His might. Put on the Whole Armor of God, that ye may be able to stand against the wiles of the devil. For we wrestle not against flesh and blood, but against principalities, against powers, against the rulers of the darkness of this world, against spiritual wickedness in high places. Wherefore take unto you the Whole Armor of God, that ye may be able to withstand in the evil day, and having done all, to stand".

—KJV
Ephesians 6:10-13, p.1474

"But God who is rich in mercy, out of the great love with which he loved us even when we were dead through our trespasses, made us alive together with Christ by grace you have been saved and raised up with him and seated us with him in the heavenly places in Jesus Christ."

—NRSV
Ephesians 2: 4-7, p. 1067

GRACE

The grace of Almighty God
Counsels and heals
With love and wisdom
Grace slowly reveals
To us our longings
To be one with His words
And soar with His angels again
In the vastness of His universe.

Grace, so undeserving, favor so sweet,
For God in His perfection,
Knows all our imperfections
And still gives us His most gracious gift,
These precious moments to live
To rename the seat of sadness
As the Mercy seat in the Tabernacle
Our lives are filled with happiness.

So the greatest honor
To Him is to live,
With happiness and health
And always with good cheer,
Knowing that His blessings
Will be beautiful, as in faith
We remember His love and kisses
When we were in Heaven's Grace.

The Holy Scriptures: It is Written

"Let us therefore approach the throne of grace with boldness so that we may receive mercy and find grace to help in the time of need."

—*NRSV*
Hebrews 4:16, p. 1108

"For the grace of God has appeared, bringing salvation to everyone, child training us to deny ungodliness and worldly desires and to live sensibly, righteously and godly in the present age."

—*KJV*
Titus 2:11-12, p. 1503

"But each of us was given grace according to the measure of Christ's gift."

—*NRSV*
Ephesians 4:7, p. 1069

My Angels Are Eternal Love

My red angel is eternal love
Who glows to create in us,

My orange angel is eternal love
Who glows to relate to us,

My yellow angel is eternal love
Who glows to assist us in study,

My green angel is eternal love
Who glows to open our hearts to one another,

My blue angel is eternal love
Who glows to tell secrets of the ages,

My violet angel is eternal love
Who glows to connect us to one another,

My purple angel is eternal love
Who glows to crown us with the glory of God.

My angels are eternal love
Who glow as hues in Heavens rainbows,

Who assist in all aspects of our earthen lives
That we reign victorious over our metaphysical, spiritual foes.

The Holy Scriptures: It is Written

Jesus said, "Take care that you do not despise one of these little ones; for, I tell you, in heaven their angels continually behold the face of my Father in Heaven."

—*NRSV*
Matthew 18: 10-11, p. 888

"For He will command His angels concerning you to guard you in all your ways. On their hands they will bear you up, so that you will not dash your foot against a stone."

—*NRSV*
Psalm 91:11-12, p. 540

"As angels were sent by God to provide sustenance for the Lord at the end of his forty days in the wilderness. Then the devil left Him and suddenly angels came and waited on Him."

—*NRSV*
Matthew 4:11, p. 873

Sweet Silver Clouds of Truth That Send the Sacred Rain

That Send the Sacred Rain

Sweet Silver Clouds of Truth
We permeate, we send
The sweet, sacred rain
We are ready to reveal,
Our innermost feelings
To replenish and to heal,
Our spirits who descend
Upon the Earth to strengthen,
To nourish for
Our relationships are new births,
Our sacred conscious callings to us to come
Closer to His mystical and majestic mirth.

When we meet we beckon
Beautiful love and great lightening,
Over 1,000 different ways
Our passion is so powerful,
Over and more over
Standing under and under,
Each flash of light

Becomes the roar of our thunder,
Sounding and resounding
Forever finding,
Our secret place where
Love and light are reborn.

Sweet Silver Clouds of Truth
We permeate we send
The sweet, sacred rain
Surging wind and sun,
Our spirits are being renewed
As we become one with
The Almighty, Elohim,
And travel from heaven to
Earth's sacred school,
The lessons of the heart
Always to be learned,
So that dark nights of the soul
are never to return,

So be loved and be cleansed
Beloved of the illusion
Of separation and judgments,
And dwell in His house

As a lover of light
Sweet Silver Clouds of Truth
We permeate we send
The sweet, sacred rain.

The Holy Scriptures: It is Written

"Sanctify them through Thy Truth: Thy Word is Truth"

—KJV
John 17:17, p. 1355

But speaking the truth in love, may grow up into him in all things, which is the head, even Christ."

—KJV
Ephesians 4:15, p. 1472

"Behold thou desirest truth in the inward parts: and in the hidden part thou shalt make me to know wisdom."

—KJV
Psalm 51:6, p. 765

"He will cover you with his feathers and under his wings you will find refuge; His faithfulness will be your shield and rampart. You will not fear the terror of the night, nor the arrow that flies by day, nor the pestilence that stalks in the darkness, nor the plague that destroys at midday. A thousand may fall at your side; ten thousand at your right hand, but will not come near you. You will only observe with your eyes and see the punishment of the wicked. If you make the Most High your dwelling—even the Lord, who is my refuge, then no harm will befall you, no disaster will come near your tent."

—NRSV
Psalm 91:4-9, p. 417

My Will, Thy Will

My will, Thy will,
Let there be,
For life is full of choices
And decisions always lead,
To paths unknown in this world
But could have known before,
We ever came to Earth, to learn
Our lessons of strength, courage and amour.

My amour, Thy amour
Let there be,
My protector of happiness
Of life and liberty,
My soul enraptured in your caress
Of light and honesty,
Seeking thy true self
And loving all that comes to me.

My Gratitude, Thy Grace
Let there be,
For all are blessings from above
A contract between you and me,
That I must fulfill if I am to become
An angel of light and love,
So help me, Holy Priest, for
My path of stones is rough,
I need your hand to keep me safe
And on this holy path of Seth.

The Holy Scriptures: It is Written

"And we know that to them that all things work together for good, to them that love God who are called according to His purpose."

—KJV
Romans 8:28, p. 1421

"And the Spirit and the bride say, Come. And let him that heareth say, Come. And let him that is athirst come; and whosoever will, let him take the Water of Life freely."

—NIV
Revelation 22:17, p. 1939

"And Jesus put forth His hand and touched him saying, "I will; be thou clean. And immediately his leprosy was cleansed."

—KJV
Matthew 8:3, p. 1206

"For it is God which worketh in you both to will and to do of His good pleasure."

—KJV
Philippians 2:13, p. 1477

ONE DAY

I have one day
To become renowned,
To determine my destiny
To grasp my crown,
A world reborn
Of love and peace
Of beauty and brilliance,
Innocence complete.

Of music and poetry
And the art of Masters
In halls of hyacinth,
Heather and asters,
Roses, violets and
Sunflowers so sweet
And smells of sandalwood,
Fern and anise.

Of ivy covered columns
Of marble and gold
And floors made of stones
From the mother of pearl,
Of light so bright
One can only see
It with a heart filled with love
And God's purity.

Of skies of royal blue
And violet rays that sparkle
Beside the Star of David
And of Bethlehem, hearken
To the heavenly angels
Who sing his joyous songs
Of spiritual rebirth
For one day forever is dawning.

The Holy Scriptures: It is Written

"For so an entrance shall be ministered unto you abundantly into the everlasting kingdom of our Lord and Savior Jesus Christ."

—KJV
2 Peter 1: 11, p. 1531

"After this I looked, and there before me was a door standing open in heaven. And the voice I had first heard speaking to me like a trumpet said, "Come up here, and I will show you what must take place after this." At once I was in the Spirit, and there before me was a throne in heaven with someone sitting on it. And the one who sat there had the appearance of jasper and carnelian. A rainbow, resembling an emerald, encircled the throne."

—NIV
Revelation 4:1, p. 1917

"And I saw the holy city, New Jerusalem, coming down out of heaven from God, prepared as a bride adorned for her husband. And I heard a loud voice from the throne saying, "See, the home" of God is among mortels. He will dwell with them; they will be his peoples"; and God himself will be with them. He will wipe every tear from their eyes. Death will be no more; mourning and crying and pain will be no more, for the first things have passed away."

—NRSV
Revelation 21:2-4, p. 1159

SPIRIT PRAYER

Swept into a sea
Of sweet memories,
Of eyes that smile
And a heart that glows
Like the sun inside
My center shows,
The love I feel
When you are near
Or far away
Makes no difference,
For my love is eternal
Faith, no fear
Of rejection, illusion,
Its face, sincere,
And willing to give
Always to you, my dearest
Whatever is needed
To fill your chalice,
With the nectar of enlightenment
Wisdom of the ages uncovered
That you know who you are

Great Soul of the Universe,
As I've come to feed your spirit
With kindness of verse,
With good health and happiness
And abiding sacramental service.

The Holy Scriptures: It is Written

"And do not grieve the Holy Spirit of God, with which you were marked with a seal for the day of redemption. Put away from you all bitterness and wrath and anger and wrangling and slander, together with all malice, and be kind to one another, tenderhearted, forgiving one another, as God in Christ ha forgiven you."

—NRSV
Ephesians 4:30-32, p.1069

"And he said to me, "You are my servant, Israel, in whom I will be glorified." But I said, "I have labored in vain I have spent my strength for nothing and vanity; yet surely my cause is with the Lord, and my reward with my God." And now the Lord says, who formed me in the womb to be his servant."

—NRSV
Isaiah 49: 3-5, p. 658

"Create in me a clean heart, O God; and renew a right spirit within me. Restore unto me the joy of thy salvation; and uphold me with thy free spirit. Then I will teach transgressors thy ways; and sinners shall be converted unto thee."

—KJV
Psalm 51: 10-13, p. 765

SHE IS THE OCEAN

She is the Ocean, of Serendipity
Each wandering wave
Connects the ones we love,
To the highest heights
Of the holy heavens
For we know our guidance
Is from above.

She is the Ocean, of loving Life-force
Never tiring,
Always moving toward the shore,
To a new place called
Higher spiritual consciousness
To assist you in your travel
To the Divine once more.

She is the Ocean, of Holiness
Here She comforts,
You who have come to worship,
Supreme Celestial Soul,
God's Galaxies of Stars
Receive Her Kiss of Love
From Her Heavenly Lips.

She is the Ocean, of Pious Possibility
She strengthens,

Your ethereal body and mind,
She tells you to wade
In Her ever flowing waters
For renewal of love and light
You will always find.

She is the Ocean of the Rabbi's Rebirth
Of happiness,
And of good health,
Come feel how Her waves
Of sparkling starlight
Return to you spiritual renewal,
Of purity and wondrous wealth.

She is the Ocean of Tranquility
With each healing wave,
She brings perfect peace,
To calm the tempest
Of your mind's eye
As you commune with
The Seraphim of the Seas.

The Holy Scriptures: It is Written

"A door was opened in heaven: and the first voice which I heard was as it were a trumpet talking with me which said, Come up hither ... and I will shew thee things which must be hereafter, And immediately I was in the spirit, and Behold, a throne was set in heaven, and one sat on the throne. And He that sat was to look upon like jasper and sardine stone; and there was a rainbow round about the throne, in sight like unto an emerald, and round about the throne were four and twenty seats: and upon the seats I saw four and twenty elders sitting clothed in white raiment; and they had crowns of gold. And out of the throne proceeded lightenings and thunderings and voices; and there were seven lamps of fire burning before the throne the which were seven spirits of God. And before the throne there was a sea of glass like unto crystal: and in the midst of the throne and round about the throne were four beasts full of eyes before and behind."

—KJV
Revelation 4:1-6, pp.1547-1548

"They shall see his face; and His name shall be on their foreheads."

—KJV
Revelation 22:4, p. 1565

THE HOLY DOVE

I want you to take my soul with a kiss
My dying breath and leave my lips
Full of faith and warmest passion
And return to the ocean my bluest ashes,

Of my sins and my sanctity
My jealousy and pain
My loving and my longing
My everlasting rays,

Of blue light and of green
For spirit of the heart
And violet and purple
The highest of the Ark,

Of Your Holy Covenant
I want to keep always
Your precious Holy Name
Forever will I praise,

Incarnation of the Supreme Being
I hope to see Your Face
Oh Heavenly Father, hear me
I beg you to forgive,

Me for my wretchedness
My decisions of sin and secrets
So foolish I found myself
Trying to hide my every weakness,

I'm begging you, oh please
Let me see your Holy Face
So undeserving I am
To kneel before Your Grace,

And gain my crown of love
As an angel in your heavenly court
I will fill my crown with jewels of peace and joy
From your precious Holy Dove.

The Holy Scriptures: It is Written

"As soon as Jesus was baptized, he went up out of the water. At that moment heaven was opened, and he saw the Spirit of God descending like a dove and lighting on him."

—NIV
Matthew 3:16p. 1499

"John bore witness, saying: I viewed the Spirit coming down as a Dove out of Heaven, and it remained upon him. Even I did not know Him, but the very One who sent me to baptize in water, said to me, Whoever it is upon whom you see the Spirit coming down and remaining, this One that baptizes in the Holy Spirit."

—NWT
John 1:32-33, p. 1328

"Greet one another with an holy kiss. All the saints salute you."

—KJV
2 Corinthians 13:12-13, p. 1461

MEDICINE WOMAN

I've searched the sky
And searched the ground,
And I have found
The greatest love renown,
From past lives
Of dry desert sands,
And mystical moons
And ancient chants,

Of starlit nights
And solemn cries,
Of the lone white wolf
And spirit eagle flights,
Of buffalo hunts
The grandmothers' voices,
Running with the wolves
And the warrior-wild horses,

Of hanging mandalas
And weaving bowls and baskets,
Holy sanctuaries
And crystal daydream catchers,
Of sacred animal calls
For each winter's survival,
And prayer for spiritual rebirth
A new spring revival,

Of wildflower blossoms
And mystical meadows of green,
Of lapis lazuli lakes
And rolling rivers of aventurine,

A sun of golden citrine
A moon of crescent diamonds,
And stars of Apache tears
That twinkle with each blink of an eye,

I reach inside myself
For this knowledge of ole,
And experience the love I forgot
One day when my heart closed,

Trying to rid myself
Of unhappiness and pain,
It is a part of my spiritual journey
So I go forth as I am ordained.

The Holy Scriptures: It is Written

"You have not chosen me, but I have chosen you, and ordained you, that you should go and bring forth fruit, and that your fruit should remain: that whatsoever ye shall ask of the Father in my name, he may give it to you."

—*KJV*
John 15:16, p. 1352

"Strengthening the souls of the disciples, encouraging them to remain in the faith and saying: "We must enter into the kingdom of God through tribulations".

—*NWT*
Acts 14:22, p. 1382

Jesus said, before He comes we are to "Go ye into all the world, and preach the good news to all creation,"

—*NWT*
Mark 16:15, p. 1282

"On the last day of the Festival, the great day, while Jesus was standing there, He cried out, "let anyone who I s thirsty come to me, and let the one who believes in me drink. As the Scripture has said, out of the believer's heart shall flow rivers of living water.

—*NRSV*
John 7:37-38, p. 966

Prayer for Wisdom and Understanding

We ask You, Lord, Your Omniscient
To grant unto us
Divine Providence and understanding,
Wisdom and courage to see the Truth
That we see beauty in all things
And that compassion be
Bestowed upon us each blessed day.

For wisdom is the key
That comes from above,
Through prayer and supplication
A meeting of the souls
And the mind's eye of ole
To heal and forgive
To understand the reasons why,

To kneel to praise You,
Great Healer of the world,
For understanding comes forth
Through communication with Divine Love
As our purpose is reborn
With each new praise and prayer for your glory
For the all the things You have done for us.
Amen.

The Holy Scriptures: It is Written

"For dominion belongs to the Lord and he rules over the nations"

—NRSV
Psalm 22:28, p. 501

"He changes times and seasons, deposes kings and sets up kings; he gives wisdom to the wise and knowledge to those who have understanding."

—NRSV
Daniel 2:21; 4:17, p. 784

And he said to him, "very truly, I tell you," you will see heaven opened, and the angels of God ascending and descending upon the Son of man."

—NRSV
John 1:51, p. 959

"The city had no need of the sun, neither of the moon, to shine in it: for the glory of God did lighten it and the Lamb is the light thereof. And the nations of them which are saved shall walk in the light of it; and the kings of the earth do bring their glory and honour into it."

—KJV
Revelation 21:23-24, p. 1565

A Gift of Dreams and Visions

Dreams are of light
And dreams are of song,
Some are of the night
And some are of the dawn,

Of sun and precious rain
Great happiness and pain,
Of fears and faith,
Of gratitude and grace,

Wisdom from the loved ones
Who have gone to heaven's home,
And premonitions of happiness
Of those whom
Are about to return to Earth,

Spirits of unity from one generation to the next
To continue the legacy of power and prayer,
Great visions of a wonderful world of perfect peace
Of waterfalls flowing to royal rivers so deep,

Of majestic mountains of purple and amethyst
Victorious valleys of golden chariots

To see the Earth from the Holy Heavens
A great gift that is complete,

So thank you, Lord for this precious gift
For each night that I kneel,
And close my eyes to pray I lift
Then fall to sleep and to hear,

Music from the upper room
Calling me to come and listen to His message,
Of love and light
And feel His Omnipresence,

For it is only a dream
A vision that only I can see,
His great and powerful majesty
Riding upon his horse of radiant beauty,

And eyes of diamonds and ruby, red fire
Brightness beyond compare,
I could see it in a vision, a dream
But only with a soul serene,

So pray each night to join
Me in my heavenly quest,
To hear his holy words of faith
And celestial songs of praise.

The Holy Scriptures: It is Written

"And it shall come to pass afterward, that I will pour out my spirit upon all flesh, and your sons and your daughters shall prophesy, your old men shall dream dreams, your young men shall see visions."

—*NRSV*
Joel 2: 28, p. 1144

"The city does not need the sun or the moon, to shine in it, for the glory of God gives it light, and the Lamb is its lamp. The nations will walk by its light, and the kings of the earth will bring their splendor into it."

—*NIV*
Revelation 21:23-24, p. 1938

"The Lord came down [from heaven] to see the city and the tower they were building."

—*NIV*
Genesis 11:5, p. 16

"As they were walking along and talking together, suddenly a chariot of fire and horses of fire appeared and separated the two of them, and Elijah went up to heaven in a whirlwind."

—*NIV*
2 Kings 2:11, p. 571

YOUR LOVE FOR GOD

Your love for God is
God's love for you,
Your longing for God is
God's longing for you,
Your connection to God is
God's connection to you,
Your wisdom of God is
God's wisdom for you,
Your need for God is
God's need for you,
Your praise for God is
God's praise for you,
Your path to God is
God's path to you,
So love and be loved,
As I am love, the Beloved.

The Holy Scriptures: It is Written

And he dreamed that there was a ladder set up on earth, the top of it reaching to heaven, and the angels of God were "ascending and descending" on it.

—NRSV
Genesis 28:12, p. 49

"He bowed the heavens and came down. Thick darkness was under his feet. He rode on a cherub, and flew; he was seen upon the wings of the wind."

—NRSV
2 Samuel 22:10-11, p. 305

"Love is patient and kind; love is not envious or boastful or arrogant or rude. It does not insist on its own way; it is not irritable or resentful; it does not rejoice in wrongdoing, but rejoices in the truth. It bears all things, believes all things, hopes all things, endures all things."

—NRSV
1 Corinthians 13: 4-7, p. 1043

Paradox of the Divine

With each decision we make,
There is always another
Way in or way out,
Which shortens or which lengthens
Our holy path to the Divine,

For Life is but a mystery
To be discovered over lifetimes
Of trials and tribulations
And hopes and exaltations,

Of love's Supreme Being
Guiding us along the path,
Ever expanding and unfolding
His gifts to us always,
Ever everlasting.

The Holy Scriptures: It is Written

"On the other hand, the fruitage of the spirit is love, joy, peace, long suffering, kindness, goodness, faith. Against such things there is no law."

—NWT

Galatians 5: 22-23, p. 1456

"For everything his an appointed time, even a time for every affair under the heavens:
A time for birth, and a time to die; a time to plant and a time to uproot what was planted; a time to kill and a time to heal, a time to break down and a time to build, a time to weep and a time to laugh; a time to wail and a time to skip about; A time to throw stones away and a time to bring stones together, a time to embrace and a time to keep away from embracing; A time to seek and a time to give up as lost; a time to keep and a time to throw away; A time to rip apart and a time to sew together; a time to keep quiet and a time for speak; A time to love and a time to hate; a time for war and a time for peace. What advantage is there for the doer in what he is working hard at?"

—NWT

Ecclesiastes 3: 1-9, p. 874

Soul Discovery

I have discovered
That the joy of laughter
· Is healing to the soul
Like no other medicine
That the world could hold
Tis something that has to be
Recognized for the self.

I have discovered
That silence can be joy
That silence can be pain
If I know who I am
Without a word of praise
Or without a word of criticism
When I make the best decisions
With mindful and soulful knowledge I possess
At that moment in time.

I have discovered
My soul's greatest desire
Is to be no other
Than whom I am
And will remain
The essence of love
That flows forever to You, My Beloved.

The Holy Scriptures: It is Written

"I want you to know, brothers that the gospel I preached, is not something that man made up. I did not receive it from any man, nor was I taught it; rather, I received it by revelation from Jesus Christ."

—*NRSV*
Galatians 1:11-12, p. 1462

"Pursue love and strive for the spiritual gifts, and especially that you may prophesy. For those who speak in a tongue do not speak to other people but to God; for nobody understands them, since they are speaking mysteries in the Spirit. On the other hand, those who prophesy speak to other people for their upbuilding and encouragement and consolation. Those who speak in a tongue build up themselves, but those who prophesy build up the church. Now I would like all of you to speak in tongues, but even more to prophesy. One who prophesies is greater than one who speaks in tongues, unless someone interprets, so that the church may be built up."

—*NRSV*
1 Corinthians 14:1-5, p. 1043

Awaken To Divine Paradox

All things contain its opposite
To keep us balanced and whole
Recognizing our true natures
That we often find:

Our faith in times of fear
Our boldness in times of meekness,
Our sadness in times of cheer
Our strength in times of weakness,

Our clarity in times of confusion
Our ego in times of blame,
Our truth in times of illusion
Our glory in times of shame,

Our love in times of hate
Our lunacy in times of sanity,
Our choices in time of fate
Our humility in times of vanity,

Our victory in times of defeat
Our life-force in times of rest,
Our joy in times of grief
Our God in times of spiritual quest.

So, awaken to Divine Providence
And duplicitous paradox
The duality of life's wonders
And serendipitous experience,
For, in the physical and spiritual
We emerge to embrace
The white rose of piety, purity
And existential grace.

The Holy Scriptures: It is Written

"They promise them freedom, while they themselves are salves of depravity—for a man is a slave to whatever has mastered him."

—NIV
2 Peter 2:19, p. 1895

"But God, being rich in mercy, because of His great, passionate love with which He loved us, even when we were dead in our transgression, made us alive together with Christ (by grace you have been permanently saved)."

—NRSV
Ephesians 2:4-5, p. 1067

"My grace is sufficient for thee for my strength is made perfect in weakness. Most gladly therefore will I rather glory in my infirmities, that power of Christ may rest upon me."

—NRSV
2 Corinthians 12:9, p. 1460

Heaven Remembered

Do you remember the love bird songs
Before the words were written?
Do you remember your lover's hand
Before you knew you were smitten?

Do you remember the sweet fragrance of roses
Before rosebuds ever bloomed?
Do you remember visions of sunsets
Before you came to Earth School?

Do you remember the songs of angels
Before you heard them in dreams?
Do you remember the taste of honey
Before the honeybee?

All are memories of our home called Heaven
Where spirits soar as angels,
As messengers of God's love and wisdom
His holy word's creation.

The Holy Scriptures: It is Written

"After this I looked, and there before me was a door standing open in heaven. And the voice I had first heard speaking to me like a trumpet said, "Come up here, and I will show you what must take place after this." At once I was in the Spirit, and there before me was a throne in heaven with someone sitting on it. And the one who sat there had the appearance of jasper and carnelian. A rainbow, resembling an emerald, encircled the throne."

—*NIV*
Revelation 4:1, p. 1917

"Ye shall see heaven open, and the angels of God ascending and descending upon the Son of man."

—*NIV*
John 1:51, p. 1648

"I will remember the deeds of the Lord. Yes, I will remember the miracles of long ago."

—*NIV*
Psalm 77.11, p. 914

I Must Prepare

I must prepare my eyes to see
A new and glorious vision,
I must prepare my ears to hear
New words from the Almighty in heaven.

I must prepare my heart to emanate love
And be open to God's miracles,
I must prepare my hands to pray for peace
And be used in God's glorious plan.

I must prepare my mind to know God
And teach His inspired words of grace,
I must prepare my lips to speak
Of His love and the power of His embrace.

The Holy Scriptures: It is Written

"And to the angel of the church in Sardis write: `The words of him who has the seven spirits of God and the seven stars. "`I know your works; you have the name of being alive, and you are dead. Awake, and strengthen what remains and is on the point of death, for I have not found your works perfect in the sight of my God. Remember then what you received and heard; keep that, and repent. If you will not awake, I will come like a thief, and you will not know at what hour I will come upon you. Yet you have still a few names in Sardis, people who have not soiled their garments; and they shall walk with me in white, for they are worthy. He who conquers shall be clad thus in white garments, and I will not blot his name out of the book of life; I will confess his name before my Father and before his angels. He who has an ear let him hear what the Spirit says to the churches.'

—*KJV*
Revelation 3: 1-6, p. 1546

"Do not let your hearts be troubled. Trust in God; trust also in me. In my Father's house there are many rooms; if it were not so I would have told you. And if I go and prepare a place for you, I will come back and take you to be where I am."

—*NIV*
John 14:2, p. 1675

Mantra

I am Love, as you are Love
This mantra is eternal
Listen to each chant of love
And cherish each moment's journey,

For as a messenger of light I grant
To those who wish to listen and to chant
This mantra from our memories and dreams
To someday see our Love Supreme,

I am Love, as you are Love
This mantra is forever light
That travels upon the wings of doves
Who circle our lives in silence, in flight.

I am Love, as you are Love
This mantra is for you, my Beloved One,
Remember its words of sweetest honey
And melodies of this blessed love song.

The Holy Scriptures: It is Written

So Jesus said to them, "Very truly I tell you, unless you eat the flesh of the Son of Man and drink His Blood, you have no life in you.

—*NRSV*
John 6:53, p. 965

"This is the bread that came down from heaven, not like that which your ancestors ate, and they died. But the one who eats this bread will live forever."

—*NRSV*
John 6:58, p. 965

"For with you is the fountain of life; in your light we see light."

—*NRSV*
Psalm 36: 9, p. 508

"Your word is a lamp unto my feet and a light unto my path."

—*NRSV*
Psalm 119: 105, p. 558

VISIONS OF MY HIGHER SELF

I close my earthen eyes
To see my heavenly heart,
Of rainbow colored flowers
And wondrous works of art,

Kindling my creativity
My spirit is overcome
With joy and inspiration
My musings just begun,

I step into my secret garden
Of fresh, fervent, misty ferns
And tropical, prophetic palms
Guiding me in my every turn,

For the path of life and love
Is generous and pure
I look to the celestial light
And my spirit will endure.

The Holy Scriptures: It is Written

"Thou shalt not hearken unto the words of that prophet, or that dreamer of dreams". "For the LORD your God proveth you, to know whether ye love the LORD your God with all your heart and with all your soul"

—*KJV*
Deuteronomy 13:3, p.267

"But ye, beloved, building up yourselves on your most holy faith, praying in the Holy Ghost, keep yourselves in the love of God, looking for the mercy of our LORD Jesus Christ unto Eternal Life".

—*KJV*
Jude 20-21, p.1543

SWEET SPIRIT GUIDE

There is a sweet, sweet spirit guide
Waiting to lead me to the other side
As the windows of my soul seeks
My wandering soul waits and weeps

And recalls the memories of long ago
When I felt your precious abiding love
Comforting me, surrounding me there
The fifth Heaven I believe is the place we shared.

The eternal flame consumes my soul
Of pink and green and blue and gold
And violet and white so beautiful and bright
I can only see it with my soul's soothing eyes

I long for you, you long for me
I cherish the moment I finally see
You, Supreme Spirit till we embrace, my heart of hearts
In a place where no one can touch

And feel that I have never left
This peaceful place of redemption, respite and rest
And I feel your warmest embrace welcome me home
Your holy place of peace and love and OM.

The Holy Scriptures: It is Written

"Ye shall walk after the LORD your God, and fear Him, and keep His Commandments, and obey His Voice, and ye shall serve Him, and cleave unto Him".

—KJV
Deuteronomy 13:4, pp. 267-268

"But ye, beloved, building up yourselves on your most holy faith, praying in the Holy Ghost, keep yourselves in the love of God, looking for the mercy of our Lord Jesus Christ unto eternal life. And of some have compassion, making a difference."

—KJV
Jude 1:20-22, p. 1543

"Show me your ways, O Lord, teach me your paths; guide me in your truth and teach me, for you are God my Savior, and my hope is in you all day long. Remember, O Lord your great mercy and love for they are from of old."

—NIV
Psalm 25: 4-6, p. 863

FAITH

My heart is a deep abiding ocean
Of anticipated joy and expected notions,
Of the substance of that which is unseen
Never doubted, for it is divine destiny.

But always hoped for, so it seems
"For the best", thus, my heart believes,
That someday the chalice of my soul will be
Overflowing with everlasting love and peace.

As my truth matures and expands throughout
The horizons of my spiritual life and mind,
May I accept that what is happening in my life
Is God's divine purpose in which I abide.

The Holy Scriptures: It is Written

"For in the gospel a righteousness of God is revealed, a righteousness that is by faith from first to last, just as it is written, the righteous will live by faith."

—NIV
Romans 1:17, p. 1747

"Early in the morning they left for the Desert of Tekoa. As they set out, Jehoshaphat stood and said, "Listen to me Judah and the people of Jerusalem! Have faith in the Lord your God and you will be upheld; have faith in his prophets and you will be successful." After consulting the people, Jehoshaphat appointed men to sing to the Lord and to praise him for the splendor of his holiness as they went out at the head of the army, saying: "Give thanks to the Lord, for this love endures forever."

—NIV
2 Chronicles 20: 20-21, pp. 701-702

"Then the disciples came to Jesus in private and asked, "Why couldn't we drive it out?" He replied, "Because you have so little faith. I tell you the truth, if you have the faith as small as a mustard seed, you can say to this mountain, move from here to there and it will move. Nothing will be impossible for you."

—NIV
Matthew 17: 19-20, p. 1525

HOPE

Hope for all things noble and new
Cherish ideals in their truest forms,
Of love, wisdom and purest thoughts
We ascend victorious, faithful and strong.

For Heaven's architects are its divine dreamers
Human hearts with universal visions,
Of beauty and endless blessedness
And everlasting life's spiritual gifts.

So to the composer, sculptor
And the wisdom of the sage,
To the poet, painter,
Prophet and musician,

Thank you for these gifts
Of holy words and visions
And sacred music as it resounds
From the mountains of Highest Heaven.

The Holy Scriptures: It is Written

And may the God of hope, fill you with every variety of joy and peace in the process of believing, unto your abounding in hope by the inherent strength from the Holy Spirit.

—NIV
Romans 15:13, p. 1767

Your hands made me and formed me, give me understanding to learn your commands. May those who fear you rejoice when they see me, for I have put my hope in your word.

—NIV
Psalm 119: 73-74, p. 960

The mystery that has been kept hidden for ages and generations, but is now disclosed to the saints. To them God has chosen to make known among the Gentiles the glorious riches of this mystery, which is Christ in you, the hope of glory.

—NIV
Colossians 1:26-27, p.1832-1833

CHARITY

Alas it is Charity,
The gift of life and love
Without regret or reservation,
Doubt or sorrowful song,

Alas it is Charity,
That I lift my eyes to you, Lord
Despite my suffering and
Solitude and tendency to hoard,

My possessions in the physical,
Those things I can never have
From those who need them most
Now with them I freely share,

For He has given me gifts
Of infinite time and space
Knowledge of the heavenly angels
And His divine gentle grace,

I give to others these gifts
To those which are most precious
To me in this life for it is
The way to receive His holy spirit.

The Holy Scriptures: It is Written

"If I have the gift of prophecy, and can fathom all mysteries and all knowledge; and though I have a faith, that can remove mountains, and have not love [charity], I am nothing".

—*NIV*
1Corinthians 13:2, p. 1786

"And to godliness brotherly kindness; and to brotherly kindness charity."

—*KJV*
2 Peter 1:7, p. 1531

"But speak thou things which become sound doctrine: That the aged men be sober, temperate, sound in faith, in charity, in patience."

—*KJV*
Titus 2:1-2, p. 1502

Prayer for Nature, Joy and Creativity

We ask you, Your Holiness
To give unto us joy and peace
And live in present moment
That we always cherish those gifts
Which are given us each day
To enjoy, to cherish
And give praise to You,
"Perfect Copy of God's Nature"
Lord Jesus Christ.

May we continue to bless your name, Lord
The "Radiant Light of Glory",
"Lamb of God and Morning Star",
For the beauty that is above our heads
And below our feet,
As we look from side to side
Comes from You, the Awesome One,
For we know that
You are in all things.
Amen.

The Holy Scriptures: It is Written

"In the beginning God created the heavens and the earth."

—NIV
Genesis 1:1, p. 1

"Who, being in very nature of God, did not consider equality with God something to be grasped, but made himself nothing, taking the very nature of a servant, being made in human likeness. And being found in appearance as a man, he humbled himself and became obedient to death—even at the cross! Therefore God exalted him to the highest place and gave him the name that is above every name, that at the name of Jesus, every knee should bow, in heaven and on earth, and every tongue confess that Jesus Christ is Lord, to the glory of God the Father."

—NIV
Philippians 2: 6-11, p. 1827

"You are the light of the world. A city built on a hill cannot be hid. No one after lighting a lamp puts it under the bushel basket, but on the lampstand, and it gives light to all in the house. In the same way, let your light shine before others, so that they may see your good works and give glory to your Father in Heaven."

—NIV
Matthew 5:14, 16, p. 1501

LIGHTENING

All my kisses to the wind
Have returned to me in
One tremendous lightening bolt
To strengthen me within,

Like an angel in disguise
Who has come to deliver
The announcement of His coming
I lay and wait for Him as He

Calls my spirit back to a life
Of happiness and good health
Of higher cosmic consciousness
And greater spiritual wealth.

So strike often, Great, glorious power
I want to feel your astral awe
And see your flashes of heaven's light
Come down and bless us all.

The Holy Scriptures: It is Written

"There was a violent earthquake, for an angel of the Lord came down from heaven and, going to the tomb, rolled back the stone and sat on it. His appearance was like lightening, and his clothes were as white as snow."

—*NIV*
Matthew 28: 2-3, p. 1549

"So if anyone tells you, There he is, out in the desert, do not go out; or, Here he is, in the inner rooms, do not believe it. For as lightening that comes from the east is visible even in the west, so will be the coming of the Son of Man."

—*NIV*
Mathew 24:27, p. 1539

"On the twenty fourth day of the first month, as I was standing on the bank of the great river, the Tigris, I looked up and there before me was a man dressed in linen, with a belt of finest gold around his waist. His body was like chrysolite, his face like lightening, his eyes like flaming torches, his arms and legs like the gleam of burnished bronze, and his voice like the sound of a multitude."

—*NIV*
Daniel 10: 4-6, p. 1389

ROMANCING THE CLOUDS

Please, don't be angry, Mother Earth
For I'm trying to do what's best for me now,
A trip on eagle's wings, a flight you see I need
To kiss the clouds and wait and see,

What picture they'll paint for me
To be near you all, oh so soft and inviting
You seek me out each day
Wondering did I see those beautiful pictures,

You painted for me today
So I had to come a little closer
To say "Hello, how beautiful you are today"
For I miss you so,

Because so seldom do I get the chance
To see you so near
When I'm flying up here
With you all, darling dears.

The Holy Scriptures: It is Written

"You set the beams of your chambers on the waters, you make the clouds your chariot, you ride on the wings of the wind, you make the winds your messengers, fire and flame your ministers."

—NRSV
Psalm 104 3, p. 545

"As I watched in the night visions, I saw one like a human being coming with the clouds of heaven. And he came to the Ancient One and was presented before him. To him was given dominion and glory and kingship, that all peoples, nations, and languages should serve him. His dominion is an everlasting dominion that shall not pass away, and his kingship is one that shall never be destroyed."

—NRSV
Daniel 7:13-14, p. 791

"At that time they shall see the Son of man coming in a cloud with power and great glory. When these things begin to take place, stand up and lift your heads, because your redemption is drawing near."

—NIV
Luke 21: 27-28, p.1636

SOUL SCAPE

As I am floating
Upon a midnight breeze
I search for your essence
Among the spirits that I see
Calling to you, calling to you
Waiting to hear your refrain
Oh Lover, I'm here,
Let's soar together again.

We reach the Heavens
And see a radiant light
Of turquoise and lavender,
Of violet and white
Transforming our lives
With this wondrous warmth of our love
Stay with me, my Lover
In this place called our heavenly home.

Just to have you with me
Oh I've waited for so long
Why do you seem so sad
As you play our lover's song?
For it's your kiss that I've missed
And your eyes gazing in mine
That fills my heart with hopes and dreams
Wishes and spiritual wine.

The Holy Scriptures: It is Written

"For he will command his angels concerning you to guard you in all ways. On their hands they will bear you up, so that you will not dash your foot against a stone."

—NRSV
Psalm 91:11-13, p. 540

In the last days it will be, God declares, that "I will pour out of My Spirit upon all flesh: and your sons and your daughters shall prophesy, and your young men shall see visions, and your old men shall dream dreams".

—NRSV
Acts 2:17, p. 985

"Then another angel came out of the temple in heaven ..."

—NRSV
Revelations 14:17, p. 1154

"The seventh angel poured his bowl into the air, and a loud voice came out of the sanctuary from the throne, saying: "It is done".

—KJV
Revelations 16:17, p. 1559

I Am a Joyous Spirit

I am the joyous spirit
Of a distant star twinkling through the trees
Like a flaming white sparkler
That glitters forever upon a flowing stream.

I am the joyous spirit
Of a giggly cherubic child
Looking up at us from my playing
Only here to laugh and to smile.

I am a joyous spirit
Kneeling in His heavenly house
For the prayers that are sent to this holy place
Are the answers of my prayers of asking.

The Holy Scriptures: It is Written

"Blessed be the God and Father of our Lord Jesus Christ, the Father of tender mercies and the God of every variety of encouragement; the encourager of us concerning every particular pressure with the goal being that we will be able to encourage those in every variety of pressure, through the encouragement with which we have been encouraged by God."

—NRSV
2Corinthians 1:3-4, p. 1048

"Let God rise up, let his enemies be scattered; let those who hate him as smoke is driven away, so drive them away; as wax melts before the fire, let the wicked perish before God. But let the righteous be joyful; let them exult before God; let them be jubilant with joy. Sing to God, sing praises to his name; lift up a song to him who rides upon the clouds. His name is the Lord. Be exultant before him."

—NRSV
Psalm 68: 1-4, pp. 524-525

SUN

So sovereign are you, My Shimmering Star
Shining in your universe,
Commanding every soul seekers attention
To love and speak Heaven's verse.

Of fiery, brilliant omnipotent force
Giving life and soaring sustenance,
With metaphysical myths and metaphors
To partake of your vibrations and dance.

So handsome are you, My Golden Sun
Commanding all of Nature's presence,
To worship you and adore you, Prince
For we need your celestial essence.

Of loving light and pillars of flaming fire
To breathe the breath of life and spiritual power,
As you bring to each and every day
A blessing to cherish with flowers.

Of resurrected lilies and redeeming lilacs
To humble the honeysuckle dew,
To lift me and to kiss me
As I kneel to pray and cosmically reach you.

O Sun, my Prince of heavenly peace
Protect me on this blessed day,
As you raise me up with your smile of sunshine
Reaching down with your lances of golden rays.

The Holy Scriptures: It is Written

"In the beginning was the Word, and the Word was with God, and the Word was God. He was in the beginning with God. All things came into being through him, and without him not one thing came into being. What has come into being in him was life, and the life was the life of all people. The light shines in the darkness, and the darkness did not overcome it."

—NRSV
John 1: 1-5, p. 958

"Then shall the righteous shine forth as the sun in the kingdom of their Father. Who has ears to hear, let him hear."

—KJV
Matthew 13: 43, p. 1216

"For the Lord God is a sun and shield: the Lord will give grace and glory: no good thing will he withhold from them that walk uprightly. O Lord of hosts, blessed is the man that trusteth in thee."

—KJV
Psalm 84: 11, p. 788

Dew Season

I awaken at the dawning
Of another mystical morning,
And see a twinkle of dancing dew drops
Luscious as lemon lollipops,

Upon the waking morning glories
Remembering last night's sweet stories,
Told by angelic and ancient souls
Who came to visit my spirit once more,

Alas my love, another kind and precious kiss
Of cool and wet upon my longing lips,
To quench my thirst for your sweetness
But for only a moment as you're my weakness,

That has descended upon my heart's home
And captured my special peace called OM,
But filled it with the warmth of another loving heart
That lives with me forever in Heaven's celestial art.

The Holy Scriptures: It is Written

"May God give you the dew of heaven, and the fatness of the earth, and plenty of grain and wine."

—*NRSV*
Genesis 27:28, p. 47

"The Lord says to my lord, "Sit at my right hand until I make your enemies your footstool." The Lord sends out from Zion your mighty scepter. Rule in the midst of your foes. Your people will offer themselves willingly on the day you lead the forces on the holy mountains. From the womb of the morning, like dew, your youth will come to you. The Lord has sworn and will not change his mind, You are a priest forever according to the order of Melchizedek."

—*NRSV*
Psalm 110:1-4, p. 551

"I will be like the dew to Israel; he shall blossom like the lily, he shall strike root like the forests of Lebanon."

—*NRSV*
Hosea 14:5, p. 806

Prayer for the Universe

We ask you, Supreme Being
To commune with the Universe
And become a part of its vastness
That gives us Day and Night
And all things old and new.

We ask you, Great Healer
To embrace the broken hearted
So that they may be filled with hope that
Love and laughter can permeate the sadness
As each smile that was given,
Will return to caress another.

We ask you, Morning Star
To kiss every shining star
And all the planets and their mystical moons
So that all whose eyes that touch the skies will be
Filled with love, happiness and peace this day.

We ask you, True Vine
That you place the spirit of truth on our hearts
So that we may walk in that truth
And know that we have the victory
Because we are saved by your grace and mercy.
Amen.

The Holy Scriptures: It is Written

"To the general assembly and church of the firstborn, which are written in heaven, and to God the Judge of all, and to the spirits of just men made perfect."

—*KJV*
Hebrews 12:23, p. 1518

"The spirit of the Lord is upon me, because he hath anointed me to preach the gospel to the poor; he hath sent me to heal the broken-hearted, to preach deliverance to the captives, and recovering of the sight to the blind, to set at liberty them that are bruised, to preach the acceptable year of the Lord."

—*KJV*
Luke 4:18-19, p. 1282

"I am the true vine, and my Father is the husbandman,"

—*KJV*
John 15: 1, p. 1351

"I am the vine, ye are the branches: He that abideth in me, and I in him, the same bringeth forth much fruit: for without me ye can do nothing."

—*KJV*
John 15: 5, p. 1351

Love Letters to God

O Mighty God, the Most High
May I speak Your Name
With greatest Honor and Holiness of spirit
That You may be praised
By all that you have made so wondrously.

"Greater Covenant, Head of Every Man"
Your holy spirit is
What has brought me here
As I seek your face
Through my prayers and meditations,

"The First and the Last", Counselor
I am so thankful to you, Lord
To whom I ask for assistance
And guidance each day
Along my unending path.

My "Great Spiritual Rock".
I love You, Lord
For You have loved and protected me
With your shield so many times
For people always hurt and they always leave
Please don't ever leave me, Lord.
Amen.

The Holy Scriptures: It is Written

"Seeing then that we have a great high priest, that is passed into the heavens, Jesus, the Son of God, let us hold fast our profession ... Let us therefore come boldly unto the throne of grace, that we may obtain mercy, and find grace to help in time of need."

—*KJV*
Hebrews 4: 14, 16, pp. 1508-1509

"Praise be to the Lord, to god our Savior, who daily bears our burdens; Our God is a God who saves; from the Sovereign Lord comes escape from death."

—*NIV*
Psalm 68: 19-20, p. 903

"He had a dream in which he saw a stairway resting on the earth, with its top reaching to heaven, and the Angels of God were ascending and descending on it."

—*NIV*
Genesis 28:12, p. 45

EPIPHANY

His gift of life, holy and precious
Beyond what one can see,
For destined was His path
On Earth, an Epiphany.

In the East, the coming of the Magi
With gold, frankincense and myrrh,
Three wisemen bearing great gifts
For the Christ Child's regal birth.

In the West, proclaiming the miracle
When the waters were turned into wine,
And the Baptism of Jesus by John
When the Holy Dove embraced the Divine.

His brief breath of life, a wondrous revelation
Of the fulfillment of God's miracle,
Was what He performed as He lived, so
Have faith and your cup will be filled.

With knowledge and with wisdom
With love, faith and hope,
With justice, strength and charity
With a spirit of showing forth.

His loving kindness is always with us
His love and light, just a gaze away,
So look to the Holy Heavens and
Through windows of seeking souls and pray.

For the Baptism in the Holy Spirit
For the miracle of the Magi at Christmas,
For East meets West in love and peace
And celebration is always forever joyous.

The Holy Scriptures: It is Written

"They set out and there ahead of them, went the star that they had seen in the rising, until it stopped over the place where the child was. When they saw that the star had stopped, they were overwhelmed with joy. On entering the house, they saw the child with Mary his mother, and they knelt sown and paid him homage. Then, opening their treasure chests, they offered him gifts of gold, frankincense and myrrh."

—*NIV*
Matthew 2: 9-11, p. 1498

This is he who was spoken of through the prophet Isaiah: "A voice of one calling in the desert. Prepare the way for the Lord, make straight paths for him."

—*NIV*
Matthew 4: 3, p. 1499

His mother said to the servants, "Do whatever he tells you." Now standing there were six stone jars for the Jewish rites of purification, each holding twenty or thirty gallons. Jesus said to them, "Fill the jars with water." And they filled them up to the brim. He said to them, "Now draw some out, and take it to the chief steward." So they took it. When the steward tasted the water that had become wine ...

—*NRSV*
John 2: 5-11, p. 959

EMMANUEL

I have been redeemed today
For prophet said to me
To pray to God for all your blessings
He has for you today.

So I raise my eyes to the heavens
And give Hosanna holy praise,
For the message was clear to me
That Jonathan will be raised,

By my daughter as my grandbaby
Glory to God, Light of the World,
For I never thought he would come to me
As I yearned for him, he yearned for me.

Blessed be, blessed be
In Jesus the Christ, we accept grace,
With fellowship and thankfulness
For faith in the Wonderful, we will be saved.

So Great is thy faithfulness
For the precious gifts we never knew,
Before we accepted Him as Savior
Such that we can never lose

That which is truly ours
For heaven shows us Thou,
As the pains of life seem dark and dreary
These illusions will crystallize.

For that which gives us tremendous pain
Also gives soothing, spiritual rain,
Of love, forgiveness, new birth
From the windows of Heaven's gates.

The Holy Scriptures: It is Written

"She will bear a son and you are to name him Jesus, for he will save his people from their sins. All this took place to fulfill what had been spoken by the Lord through the prophet. "Behold a virgin shall conceive, and bear a son, and his name shall be called Emmanuel", which means "God is with us.""

"When Joseph awoke from sleep, he did as the angel of the Lord commanded him; he took her as his wife, but had no marital relations with her until she had borne a son; and he named him Jesus."

—NRSV
Matthew 1:21-25, p. 871

Lord, Save Us

Lord, save us from this hunger
Of precious light and thunder,
Resounding from the great universe
That no soul can place asunder.

Lord, save us from this hunger
To belong to your family of peace,
Permeating all understanding
As all heartache and hate are released.

Lord, save us from this hunger
To sow the seeds of abundance for our family,
To guard of gates of spiritual obedience to You
So we may always have good health, wealth and happiness.

Lord, save us from this hunger
Allow the valleys in our lives to remain,
So that we become forever humble in your presence
And be baptized in the waters of your holy name.

The Holy Scriptures: It is Written

"My little children, these things I am writing to you in order that you should not sin. And if anyone should sin, we continually have a helper, an advocate, in the personal presence of the Father, Jesus Christ the righteous one. He Himself is the satisfaction concerning our sins and not concerning ours only, but also concerning all the world."

—NRSV
Romans 3:23-26, p. 1020

"For while we were still weak, at the right time Christ died for the ungodly. In deed, rarely will anyone die for a righteous person—though perhaps for a good person someone might actually dare to die. But God proves his love for us in that while we still were sinners Christ died for us. Much more surely then, now that we be saved through him from the wrath of God. For if while we were enemies, we were reconciled to God through the death of his Son, much more surely, having been reconciled, will we be saved by his life."

—NRSV
Romans 10:1-13, p. 1027

Unconditional Love

Have I grown enough to accept
The fate of sorrow and grief,
If I'd say to another
My well of love is deep?

Beyond what is conceived unless
I can feel the flow,
Of love unconditional
As a heavenly glow.

Of light from the Angels
Who have come to console,
A heart that is pierced
With a loving arrow of gold.

Its purpose only to open
And to soften as I grow old,
My heart of hearts and remember
The Bridegroom, the Savior of my soul.

The Holy Scriptures: It is Written

"And I will take you for my wife forever; I will take you for my wife in righteousness and in justice, in steadfast love, and in mercy. I will take you for my wife in faithfulness; and you shall know the Lord."

—NRSV
Hosea 2:19-20, p. 799

"Then I heard what seemed to be the voice of a great multitude, like the sound of many waters and like the sound of mighty thunder-peals, crying out, "Hallelujah! For the Lord our God the Almighty reigns. Let us rejoice and exult and give him the glory, for the marriage of the Lamb has come, and his bride has made herself ready; to her it has been granted to be clothed with fine linen, bright and pure" for the fine linen is the righteous deeds of the saints."

—NRSV
Revelation 19:6-8, p. 1157

IN THE NAME OF JESUS

I look to the Holy Heavens
And see a sparkling star,
Awesome, wondrous
For these I feel you are,
Shining in your glory
And excellence in refrain,
I want to speak your name, "Lord"
"Lamb Without Spot or Stain".

"Wonderful", "Counselor"
"Prince of Life and Peace",
"Radiant Light of Glory"
"The Image of the Unseen",
"Lion of the Tribe of Judah"
As "His Words Were Made Flesh",
"The Way the Truth and the Light",
"Son of the One Blessed".

"The Only Son of the Father"
"First Born of All Creation",
"Perfect Copy of God's Nature"
"The Power of Salvation",
"Chief Shepherd, Living Bread"
"Lamb of God, Morning Star",
"Greater Covenant, Head of Every Man"
Our "Great Spiritual Rock".

"Everlasting Father, The Advocate"
"Yeshua, The Messiah,
"The First and the Last, God of Glory"
"Man, The Hidden Manna".
"The Light of the World, Rabbi"
"Redeemer, Righteous Judge",
"The Eldest of Many Brothers,
Precious Cornerstone, Chosen One".

"Lily of The Valley, Ruler of All"
"Savior, The Second Adam",
"True Vine, Hope, Inexpressible Gift"
"The Holy Rose of Sharon".
"Bridegroom, Israel's Comforting"
"Master, Lord of all Men",
"The Rising Sun, Alpha and Omega"
"The Christ, King of Kings".

The Holy Scriptures: It is Written

"For a child will be born for us, and a mature son will be given to us, and the government will rest on His shoulders, and His name will be called: Wonderful, Counselor, The Mighty God, The Everlasting Father, The Prince of Peace."

—*NRSV*
Isaiah 9:6, p. 623

"Then I saw heaven opened, and there was a white horse! Its rider is called Faithful and True, and in righteousness he judges and makes war. His eyes are like a flame of fire, and on his head are many diadems; and he has a name inscribed that no one knows but himself. He is clothed in a robe dipped in blood, and his name is called The Word of God. And the armies of heaven, wearing fine linen, white and pure, were following him on white horses. From his mouth comes a sharp sword with which to strike down the nations, and he will rule them with a rod of iron; he will tread the wine press of the fury of the wrath of God the Almighty. On his robe and on his thigh he has a name inscribed, "King of kings and Lord of lords."

—*NRSV*
Revelation 19:11-16, p. 1158

REDEMPTION

My sins have overcome me, Lord
I am filled with guilt and shame,
So I stay away from your holy house
For I had made you a promise
Ago many yesterdays,
To do everything that asked of me
But my prayer was not answered,
So very lonely I felt,
That the Holy stones
Of the Ten Commandments
Had become broken promises
And disenchantments,
Deceptions, half truths, disillusionments
Of my own human perfections
So my heart was led astray
For the love I desired from someone
Somehow was lost along the way.
Redeem me, Dearest Lord on this day
Please give me the assurance
That my living is not in vain
And that all that seemed to have been lost
Was truly a spiritual gain
And that I will rest in Your arms
As your child forever and always.

The Holy Scriptures: It is Written

> *Therefore, since we have a great high priest who has gone through the heavens, Jesus the Son of God, let us hold firmly to the faith we profess. For we do not have a high priest who is incapable of sympathizing with our weaknesses, since He had been tempted in a like manner in every way apart from sin. Let us then confidently approach the Throne of Grace, that we might receive mercy and find grace for help at exactly the right time."*
>
> *—NIV*
> **Hebrews 4:14-16, p. 830**

> *"At that time they shall see the Son of man coming in a cloud with power and great glory. When these things begin to take place, stand up and lift your heads, because your redemption is drawing near."*
>
> *—NIV*
> **Luke 21: 27-28, p. 1636**

LOVE SENSES

Please listen to the soothing sounds of love
As it heals your ailing ears,
Deafened by the harshness of words
And calms your inner fears.

O Look to the divine visions of love
As it heals your saddened eyes,
Blinded by jealousy and pain
Your tender tears it dries.

O Smell the flowery fragrance of love
As it heals with sacred sage,
With lilies of resurrection
And aloe of healing faith.

O Taste the sweetness of honey, love
As it heals your bitterness,
Of a heart closed to love and kindness
Acceptance and forgiveness.

Please feel the depth and breadth of love
As it heals your lonely soul,
For missing is your own heart of hearts
Filled with Sharon's Rose.

The Holy Scriptures: It is Written

"I am a Rose of Sharon" a Lily of the Valley

—NIV
Song of Songs 2:1, p. 1050

"Jesus said, "Love the Lord your God with all your heart, soul and mind." This is the first and most important commandment. The second most important commandment is like this one. And it is, "Love others as much as you love yourself." All the Law of Moses and the Books of the Prophets are based on these two commandments."

—NIV
Matthew 22: 37-39, p. 1536

"The eyes of your understanding being enlightened; that ye may know what is the hope of his calling, and what the riches of the glory of his inheritance in the saints."

—KJV
Ephesians 1: 18, p. 1469

The Precious Garden
of The Lord

A smile from above has embraced me again,
Another day from the East of Eden's garden,
How I've missed its holiness, its beauty,
If only I had listened to You, Father God,

So, if You, Father God,
Would just give me another chance,
An opportunity to see Eden again,
I pray that I will never, ever gaze,
Not ever in the direction of that tree,
For the tree from which you asked
That I shall not eat,

Now I fight, to maintain my favor,
As undeserving as it is to me,
For if I had not thought that I would be as You,
As the arrogant one said, Your Omnipotence,
A life of constancy, kindness, generosity
And Holy Guidance at every turn,

For I know I will possess
The fresh fruits of the spirit,
So my plan to journey
To the precious garden of Victory,

I will wait and wait and
Wait and wait and wait
Upon You, Father God,
Planting seed, after seed, after seed.

The Holy Scriptures: It is Written

"To the garden of nut trees I had gone down, to see the buds in the torrent valley, to see whether the vine had sprouted, whether the pomegranate trees had blossomed. Before I knew it, my own soul had put me at the chariots of my willing people."

—NWT
Song of Songs 5:11, p. 887

"The Lord God took the man and put him in the garden of Eden to till it and to keep it."

—NRSV
Genesis 2:15, p. 28

"For the grace of God has appeared, bringing salvation to everyone, child training us to deny ungodliness and worldly desires and to live sensibly, righteously and godly in the present age."

—NRSV
Titus 2:11-12, p. 1100

An Experience of Faith

How do I experience Faith
As the heavens are moving about my head?
Or is Faith making a stand
Upon the Mother Earth where we are to tread?

As Faith moves about the Heavens
Along its own holy path,
A part of God's divine vessels
Healing with every touch in a cosmic bath.

Circling as brilliant stars
Of blue, and red, and yellow,
And orange, and green, and purple fires
Burning the paths of passion and compassion,

For all who seek their celestial faces,
Embracing the spirits of another and another,
Their holy energies shared
For one brief moment to soar,

Above the physicality and limitations
The confinement of human existence,
One movement of perfect peace,
To know the true essence

Of the love and light of God,
And His wonders and amazement
That sparks these adventures of faith
That sustains us to our next spiritual adventure.

The Holy Scriptures: It is Written

"In the past God spoke to our forefathers through the prophets at many times and in various ways, but in these last days he has spoken to us by His Son, whom he appointed heir of all things, and through whom he made the universe. The Son is the radiance of God's glory and the exact representation of his being, sustaining all this by his powerful word. After he had provided purification for sins, he sat down at the right hand of the Majesty in heaven."

—NIV
Hebrews 1:1-3, p. 1862

Clearly no one is justified before God by the law, because, "The righteous will live by faith."

—NIV
Galatians 3:11, p. 1812

"In addition to all this, take up the shield of faith, with which you can extinguish all the flaming arrows of the evil one."

—NIV
Ephesians 6:16, p. 1824

"Let us fix our eyes on Jesus, the author and perfecter of our faith, who for the joy set before him endured the cross, scorning shame, and sat down at the right hand of the throne of God."

—NIV
Hebrews 12:2, p. 1877

Lord, Bring Us Peace, Hope and Understanding

As a mighty fortress,
You've come to protect us, your children of God,
In times of our terrible troubles,
As the roaring lion of Judah,
You've come to destroy,
All of the deceivers,
Of your holy word,

As we seek peace and hope for the world,
They call us the peacemakers,
Let us sow the quiet of the earth
So that we can reap the harvest of peace,
And smile upon the children of the world
That we have made a difference in their lives
And that the future is bright for them,

Please continue to give us hope,
Please bring us your joy and peace,
Please bring perfect understanding
To our hearts and minds,
So that we may go forth,
And sing the Good News,
Of your Holy and Blessed Name.
Amen.

The Holy Scriptures: It is Written

"In whom also ye also trusted, after that ye heard the word of truth, the gospel of salvation: in whom also after that ye believed, ye were sealed with that Holy Spirit of promise, which is the earnest of our inheritance until the redemption of the purchased possession, unto the praise of his glory."

—KJV
Ephesians 1:13-14, p. 1469

"For the Word of God is quick, and powerful, and sharper than any two-edged sword, piercing even to the dividing asunder of soul and spirit, and of the joints and marrow, and is a Discerner of the thoughts and intents of the heart".

—KJV
Hebrews 4:12, p. 1508

God Calls Us

God calls us to baptism
God calls us to heavenly hear,
God calls us to community
God calls us to all draw near,
God calls us to fellowship
God calls us to blessed play,
God calls us to stand for Him
God calls us to humbly pray,
God calls us to speak His word
God calls us to duty and faith,
God calls us to devote our lives to Him
God calls us to never ending divine grace,
God calls us to inspiration
God calls is to tell our story,
God calls us to complete our dedication
Then, God calls us Home to Glory.

The Holy Scriptures: It is Written

"For everything has its season, and for every action under the heaven, there is a time: A time to be born and a time to die; a time to plant and a time to uproot; A time to weep and a time to laugh; a time for mourning and a time for dancing; A time to scatter stones and a time to gather them; a time for embrace and a time to refrain from embracing; A time to seek and a time to loose; a time to keep and a time to throw away; A time to tear and a time to mend; a time for silence and a time for speech; A time to love and a time to hate; a time for war and a time for peace ... "

—KJV
Ecclesiastes 3: 1-8, p. 863

"For this reason I bow my knees before the Father from whom every family in heaven and on earth takes its name. I pray that according to the riches of his glory, He may grant that you may be strengthened in your inner being with power and grounded in love. I pray that you may have the power to comprehend, with all the saints, what is the breadth and length and height and depth, and to know the love of Christ that surpasses knowledge, so that you may be filled with all the fullness of God. Now to him by the power at work within us is able to accomplish abundantly for more than all we can ask or imagine, to Him be the glory in church and in Christ Jesus to all generations, forever and ever. Amen."

—NRSV
Ephesians 3: 14-21, p. 1068

References

1. The Holy Bible Containing the Old and New

   Testaments, King James Version (KJV), (translated out of the original tongues and with the former translations diligently compared and revised), Giant Print Reference Edition, A Regency Bible from Thomas Nelson Publishers, Inc. 1980.

2. The New Student Bible, New Revised Standard Version (NRSV), the Division of Christian Education of the National Council of Churches of Christ in the U.S.A., The Zondervan Publishing House Corporation, Grand Rapids, MI, 1994 Edition.

3. The Holy Bible, Containing the Old and New

   Testaments, New International Version (NIV), International Bible Society, The Zondervan Publishing House Corporation, Grand Rapids, MI, 1986 Edition.

4. The New World Translation of the Holy Scriptures (NWT), Rendered from the Original Languages by the New World Bible Translation Committee, Revised 1984, Watch Tower Bible and Tract Society of New York, Inc., and the International Bible Students Association, Brooklyn, NY, U.S.A. 1984.

5. Wilson, Melvinia "Cissy" Patterson, Love's Embrace: Poems of Love and Inspiration, copyright 2000, 2005, 2006.

Biography

Melvinia "Cissy" Patterson Wilson has been writing poetry and prayers for the past five years. Her pursuit of love and spiritual awareness has always been the focus of her inner life. Her writings attempt to heal those who read them, as they are written with assistance from the "Light and Love from the Angels in Heaven", and, as Jesus, the Christ, teaches us to love each other, from the holy scriptures of the Bible.

"Cissy" is a native of Richmond, Virginia and lives in the metropolitan area. She obtained a Bachelor of Arts degree in Administration/Management from Chatham College, Pittsburgh, Pennsylvania and a Master of Business Administration degree in Accounting from Atlanta University, Atlanta, Georgia. She has worked in banking, has been a college instructor, and has worked in government finance for the past 15 years. Currently, she is a doctoral candidate for a degree in Education from the Graduate Theological Foundation/Oxford, Oxford England.

She attended the University of Oxford's Summer Programme in Theology in 2004 and 2006, watched and listened to the sermons of evangelists from all over the world, as well as read some of the great commentaries throughout the centuries. All these messages from Jesus the Christ have assisted her in the writing and referencing of this book. Jesus the Christ, The Passion, has been her most recent topic of study. Other topics include visual faith through the world's major religious traditions, depictions of the Christ and the Virgin Mary, medieval religious art in Europe, and African religious art and artifacts during the Diaspora, depictions of slavery during the Middle Passage.

Her first book, <u>Love's Embrace: Poems of Love and Inspiration,</u> is a book of love dealing with mainly love of men, women and children. As her spirit grew stronger through the reading of the Holy Scriptures, searching for deeper spiritual consciousness and the pursuit of global peace, she birthed this book, <u>Loves Embrace: Poems of Prayer, Hope and Peace.</u>

She states, "Once love finds its way to your heart and soul, it begins to permeate throughout your life and to those you love, for you never stop loving, as it is a continuation of God's love for all of us. Here we have to find the source of life and continuous harmony. With divine purpose, God's grace and inspirational poetry as the instrument, with the assistance of the Holy Spirit, I have tried to gift you with the "Word of God". I hope you have been blessed with inspiration and peace, for now the world knows my heart, and my heart is very well pleased."

The Spirit and the bride say, "Come!" And let him who hears say "Come!" Whoever is thirsty, let him come, and whoever wishes, let him take the free gift of the water of life.

—NIV
Revelation 22: 17, p. 861

For God so loved the world that He gave His only begotten Son, that whosoever believeth in Him shall not perish but have everlasting life.

—KJV
John 3:16, p. 1328

About the Author

Melvinia "Cissy" Patterson Wilson has been writing poetry and prayers for the past five years. Her pursuit of love and spiritual awareness has always been the focus of her inner life. Her writings attempt to heal those who read them, as they are written with assistance from the "Light and Love from the Angels in Heaven", and, as Jesus, the Christ, teaches us to love each other, we hopefully will receive the blessings He wants to bestow upon us.

"Cissy" is a native of Richmond, Virginia and lives in the metropolitan area. She obtained a Bachelor of Arts degree in Administration/Management from Chatham College, Pittsburgh, Pennsylvania and a Master of Business Administration degree in Accounting from Atlanta University, Atlanta, Georgia. She has worked in banking, has been a college instructor, and has worked in government finance for the past 15 years. Currently, she is a doctoral candidate for a degree in Education from the Graduate Theological Foundation/Oxford, Oxford England and South Bend, Indiana.

978-0-595-44655-1
0-595-44655-8

www.ingramcontent.com/pod-product-compliance
Lightning Source LLC
Chambersburg PA
CBHW051246050326
40689CB00007B/1080